RON MILLER

SATURN

WORLDS BEYOND

TWENTY-FIRST CENTURY BOOKS   BROOKFIELD, CONNECTICUT

Dedicated to Natalie Grace Luffman

Illustrations by Ron Miller. Photographs courtesy of NASA.

Library of Congress Cataloging-in-Publication Data
Miller, Ron, 1947-
Saturn / Ron Miller.
p. cm. — (Worlds beyond)
Summary: Chronicles the discovery and exploration of the planet Saturn and discusses its rings and moons, its place in the solar system, and more.
Includes bibliographical references and index.
ISBN 0-7613-2360-0 (lib. bdg.)
1. Saturn (Planet)—Juvenile literature. [1. Saturn (Planet)] I. Title. II Series.
QB671 .M56 2003   523.46—dc21   2002014098

Published by Twenty-First Century Books
A Division of The Millbrook Press, Inc.
2 Old New Milford Road
Brookfield, Connecticut 06804
www.millbrookpress.com

CONTENTS

The astronomical symbol for Saturn

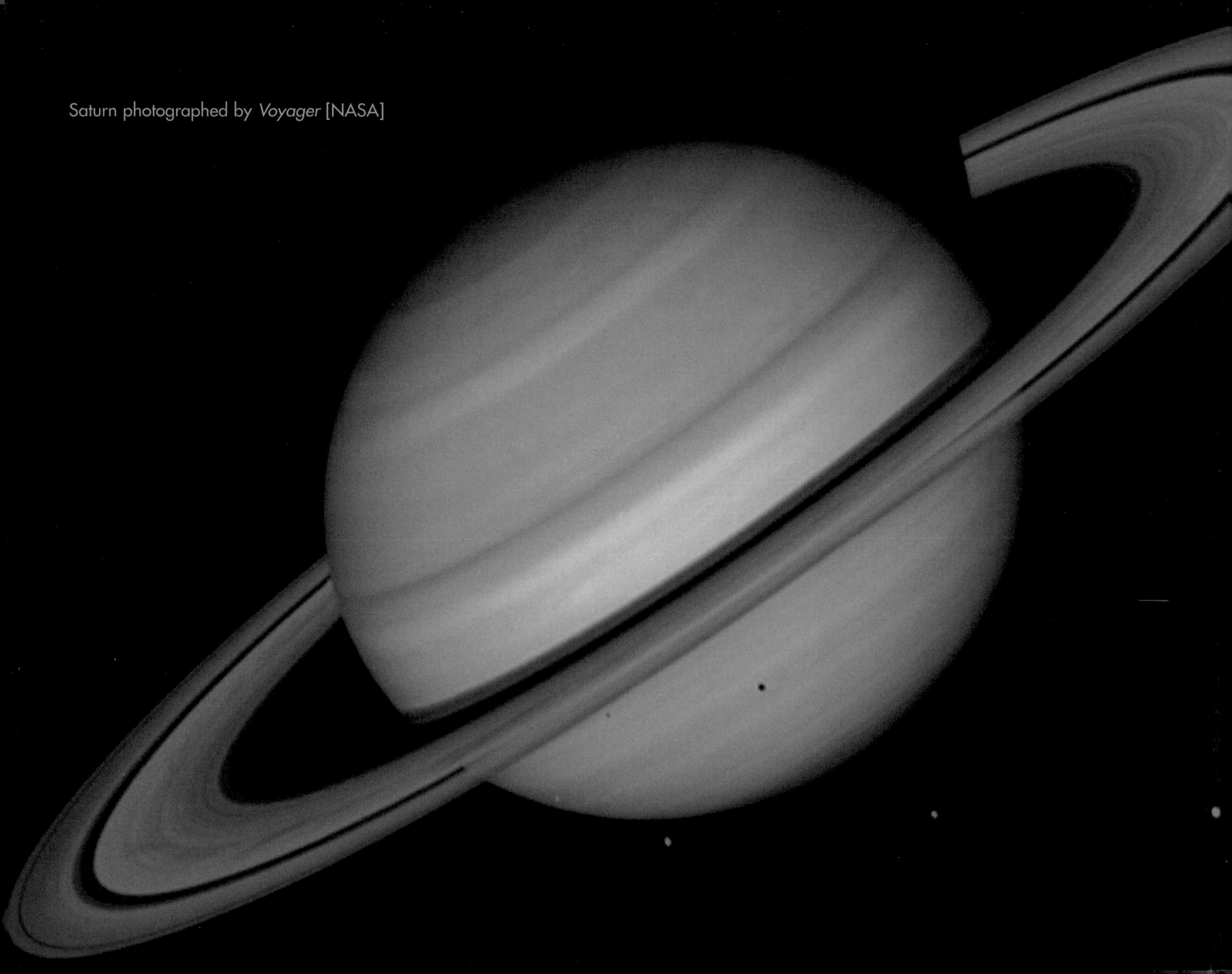
Saturn photographed by *Voyager* [NASA]

CHAPTER ONE

LORD OF THE RINGS

Glowing a dull yellow in the night sky, Saturn is the slowest-moving of the five planets known to the ancients. Representing age and the passage of time, it was named for the Roman god of Time and Destiny. In Roman mythology, Saturn was the father of Jupiter, while Jupiter was the father of Mars, Venus, Mercury, and the Sun. For the first people to observe the night sky many thousands of years ago until those at the end of the eighteenth century, Saturn's **orbit** marked the extreme limit of our solar system's realm. Even to Galileo, Copernicus, and Newton, Saturn was the farthest known planet.

Until just four hundred years ago, however, no one knew that the sluggish yellow star *was* a planet—at least, not in the sense that we use the word today. It was just one of five stars that were no different from any others except that—unlike all of the thousands of fixed stars—they slowly moved through the sky.

Discovering Planets

Thousands of years ago, everyone watched the stars. Keeping track of their movements was important to daily life. So of course it was quickly noticed if anything strange or unusual occurred among them. While stars have always differed in brightness and color, they were all fixed motionless in the sky. The same stars always appeared in the same relationship to one another, night after night. All except for five. These strange stars changed position from night to night. The difference was very slight because they move very slowly—it takes days, weeks, or even months to notice the movement—but they do move. The Greeks named these moving stars *planetes*, which means "wanderers."

An astronomer of the second century with his instruments

Although the word *planet* was originally Greek, the names of the planets themselves come from Roman mythology. The five planets known in ancient times were named after the five most important Roman gods. Mercury was named for the messenger of the gods, since it is the swiftest-moving planet; Venus after the goddess of love and beauty, because her star was so bright and lovely to look at; Mars, the red planet, was named for the god of war; Jupiter, the brightest of the planets to appear in the sky all night, was named for the chief of all the gods; and Saturn, of course, was named for the god of time.

As interesting as the planets were, they were not thought to be anything particularly special. No one ever considered the possibility that they might in fact be other *worlds*. Not until the year 1610, that is.

The Italian scientist Galileo Galilei had been experimenting with an amazing new optical instrument that had been recently invented in the Netherlands. It consisted of nothing more than a pair of ordinary glass lenses set at either end of a wooden tube, but it had the remarkable property of making distant objects appear closer. The Dutch were immediately aware of its potential use to navigators and the military, and this was Galileo's first impression, too. But then he did something with the telescope that no one had thought of doing: He turned it toward the night sky.

Galileo quickly made an astonishing discovery. While the rest of the stars in the sky looked like brilliant points of light when seen through his telescope, the five planets looked like tiny disks. Venus showed phases like the Moon, proving that it was spherical

The mythological Roman god Saturn

A nineteenth-century engraving of Galileo demonstrating his first telescope

and circled the Sun. Mars showed dusky patches that he thought might be continents and seas. Jupiter had four tiny **satellites** of its own, like a miniature solar system, and Saturn . . . well, Saturn was a complete mystery.

Galileo's telescope was small and not very powerful. It was not even as strong as a modern pair of binoculars. He couldn't see Saturn quite well enough to make out any details, but he could see it just enough to realize that there was something very strange about the planet. To him, it appeared as though it were a triple planet: a large one with two smaller ones touching on either side. Galileo racked his brain for an explanation, but was completely stumped. While he waited for someone else to come up with an explanation, he put his discovery in the form of a cryptogram: SMAISNERMAILMBPOETALEUMVNEUVGTTAVIRAS. Scientists often did this in Galileo's time when they wanted to protect the precedence of a discovery without actually giving away what they had discovered. When properly rearranged, the list of letters formed the Latin phrase "*Altissimum planetam tergeminum observavi,*" which means, "I have observed that the farthest planet is triple."

"When I observe Saturn," Galileo wrote to the Grand Duke of Tuscany, "the central star appears the largest; two others, one situated to the east, the other to the west . . . seem to touch it. They are like two servants who help old Saturn on his way, and always remain at his side."

Unable to solve the mystery of the triple planet, Galileo turned his attention to other studies. When he observed Saturn two years later, in 1612, he was met with an even greater mystery: the two extra globes were missing! He had no idea what to make

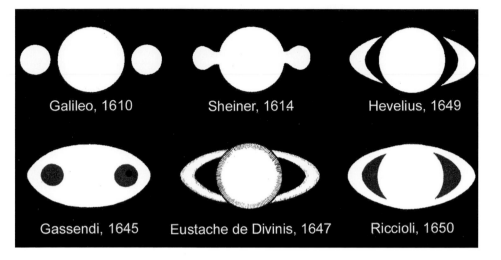

Galileo, 1610

Sheiner, 1614

Hevelius, 1649

Gassendi, 1645

Eustache de Divinis, 1647

Riccioli, 1650

of this and, in despair, took no further interest in Saturn. He died without ever learning Saturn's secret.

In 1655, a twenty-six-year-old astronomer named Christian Huygens observed Saturn with a much better telescope. He also made an exciting discovery and, like Galileo, first published it in the form of a strange list of letters: AAAAAA, CCCCC, D, EEEEE, G, H, IIIIIII, LLLL, MM, NNNNNNNN, OOOO, PP, Q, RR, S, TTTTT, UUUUU. Three years later, he revealed that these letters could be rearranged to spell the Latin phrase "*Annulo cingitur tenui plano, nusquam cohaerente, ad eclipticam inclinato,*" which means, "It is surrounded by a thin flat ring, not attached to the body at any point, and inclined to the **ecliptic**."

Huygens had discovered three fundamental facts about the nature of Galileo's mystery planet: It is surrounded by a flat ring, the ring does not touch the planet, and the ring is inclined to the

Christian Huygens

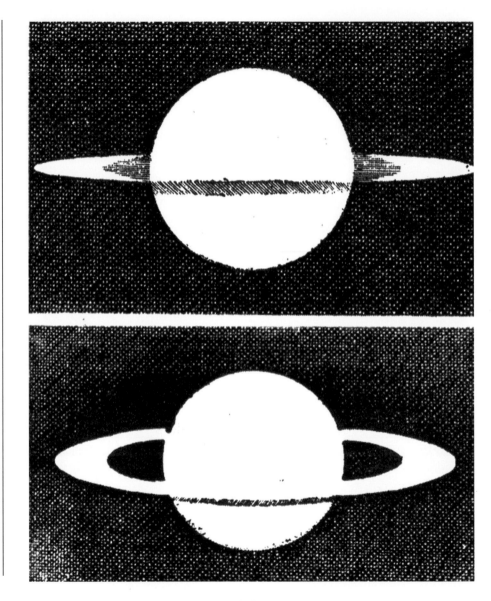

A drawing published by Christian Huygens in 1655 illustrates his discovery of the true nature of Saturn's rings: a flat band encircling the planet, touching it nowhere.

(10)

plane of the ecliptic (that is, it is tipped in relation to the plane of Earth's orbit). The ecliptic is the plane in which Earth orbits. Imagine the ecliptic as being a broad flat disk and the planets as small balls rolling around on it. Most of the planets orbit nearly in the same plane as Earth. The planets themselves, however, can be tipped in relation to the ecliptic. Earth's axis, for instance, is tipped about 23 degrees to the plane of the ecliptic. Saturn's is tipped even more, at 27 degrees.

As Saturn orbits the Sun, the rings are sometimes tipped toward Earth and sometimes they are tipped away from Earth, which means that sometimes we can see their upper or lower surface, and sometimes they are presented edge-on. When the latter occurs, the rings, which are extremely thin, seem to vanish. This happens every fifteen years and explains why Galileo's two extra globes disappeared.

Further discoveries about Saturn came quickly. In addition to his discovery of the true nature of the rings, Huygens also found that Saturn had a moon orbiting it every two weeks. This moon was later named Titan. Huygens might have discovered some of the other satellites, but stopped looking after he found the first one since he did not believe that there would be any others. "As there are but six planets," he explained, "there can exist but six satellites"—Earth had one, Jupiter four, and Saturn one.

In 1675, Jean Dominique Cassini—an Italian astronomer who had moved to France at the invitation of King Louis XIV to supervise the new Paris Observatory—observed that the rings were divided by a thin, dark line. He realized that this meant there were two distinct rings separated by a gap. Today, the outer ring is

Jean Dominique Cassini

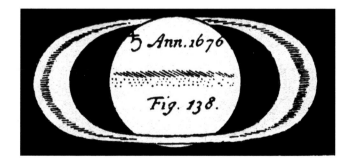

This original drawing by Cassini shows the gap in the rings that was later named for him.

(11)

Saturn's moons actually weren't officially named until the early nineteenth century. Cassini had wanted to name the moons he had discovered after his patron, Louis XIV, but the idea wasn't very popular with astronomers from other countries. Instead, Sir John Herschel (the son of Sir William Herschel, the discoverer of Uranus) suggested naming the moons after the Titans and Giants, who were the brothers and sisters of Cronus, the Greek equivalent of Saturn. The first two moons to be named, which were discovered by Sir William Herschel, were called Mimas and Enceladus. Then came Tethys, Dione, Rhea, Titan, Hyperion, and Iapetus. Saturn is now known to have at least thirty moons.

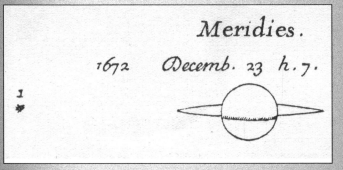

This drawing by Cassini shows his discovery of Rhea, the "star" at the far left, in 1672.

called the A ring, the inner, brighter ring is the B ring, and the gap between them is called the Cassini division. Cassini also discovered four more satellites: Iapetus in 1671, Rhea in 1672, and Dione and Tethys in 1684, which must have come as a big surprise to Huygens.

Soon, other astronomers discovered additional gaps in the rings. German astronomer Johann Franz Encke found one in 1837, dividing the outer ring into two parts, and Father F. de Vico, the director of the Collegio Romano Observatory in Italy, found several gaps in the main ring. In 1850, Americans William C. Bond and George P. Bond and Englishman William Rutter Dawes discovered an entirely new ring inside the two previously known ones. This ring was called the "crêpe ring" because it is so thin and transparent that it resembles crêpe paper.

The Mysterious Rings

The earliest observers of Saturn didn't know what to make of the rings. What could they be? Most assumed that they were solid, like a disk cut from a sheet of paper. Cassini thought they consisted of a swarm of countless millions of individual particles, but his idea was pretty much ignored. In 1795, the French mathematician Pierre-Simon Laplace calculated that a solid ring was impossible. It would have to be broken up by the gravitational forces of Saturn. His idea—inspired by the existence of the Cassini division—was that the rings were divided into a great many very narrow, concentric rings, each separated from the other by narrow gaps too small to be seen through telescopes. In other words,

Saturn's rings were like thousands upon thousands of individual, solid hoops. Laplace's idea was accepted for nearly half a century.

Sir William Herschel spent a great deal of time observing Saturn in the late eighteenth century. He was the first to suggest that the rings were extremely thin, perhaps no more than 300 miles (500 km) thick. This might not sound very thin until you consider them in proportion to the rings' vast width: 146,000 miles (235,000 km) from one edge of the A ring to the other. (Today we know that the rings are even thinner than Herschel supposed.)

The discovery of the inner crêpe ring in 1850 proved that the rings could not be solid, since the new ring was transparent—Saturn was clearly visible through it. If they were not solid, what could they be? Some astronomers suggested that the rings were some sort of liquid, while others thought they might be made of gas.

In 1848, the French mathematician Édouard Roche calculated that if a large satellite were to approach too closely to a large planet, the satellite would be torn apart by **tidal forces** caused by the planet's gravity. This happens because the gravitational pull of a planet on a moon is not equal all around. The planet pulls more on the side of the moon closest to it and less on the side farther away. If the moon gets too close, this unequal pull can become great enough to tear the moon apart. Every planet has what is called a **Roche limit**, within which a large satellite cannot come without being pulled into pieces. Likewise, bits of material orbiting a planet within the Roche limit will never be able to pull

William Herschel

A drawing of Saturn by John Browning, a nineteenth-century British astronomer

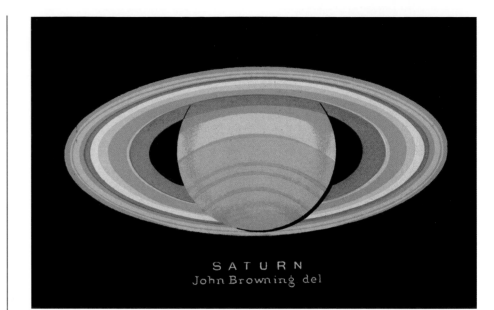

SATURN
John Browning del

themselves into the form of a moon. Roche realized that Saturn's rings lay within the Roche limit of the planet and suggested that they might have formed when a satellite wandered too closely to Saturn and was destroyed.

The nature of Saturn's rings was finally settled in 1857 through a contest held by the University of Cambridge, in England. It had offered a prize for the best essay "to determine the extent to which the stability and appearance of Saturn's rings would be consistent with alternative opinions about their nature, whether they are rigid or fluid, or made up of masses of matter not mutually coherent. . . ."

The prize essay was written by James Clerk Maxwell, a young Scottish physicist. He showed that even the thinnest solid ring would be torn apart by tidal forces. According to his calculations, the rings could only be a vast number of tiny, individual moonlets, each in its own independent orbit. Seen from the distance of Earth, the millions of little particles gave the appearance of a solid ring. (You can see for yourself how the individual particles can give the appearance of a solid ring when seen from a distance. A photograph in a newspaper looks like continuous tones of gray, but when you look at it closely, you can see that it is really made up of thousands of individual, separate dots.)

Maxwell's theory was proven correct in 1895 by James E. Keeler, who used a **spectroscope** to measure the rotation speed of different parts of the ring. He found that the inner parts of the ring rotated much faster than the outer parts, just as one would expect if the rings were made up of individual particles. If they had been solid, the outer rim would rotate faster than the inside (as when the wheel of a bicycle rotates, the rim moves more quickly than the hub).

As fascinating as the rings were, astronomers did not ignore the planet itself. Studying Saturn was still not easy, however. Although it is a very large planet—more than nine times larger than Earth—it is also very far away, much farther away than Jupiter. Astronomers could see that the surface of Saturn had bands like Jupiter, though much fainter, and occasional bright white spots, but that was about all.

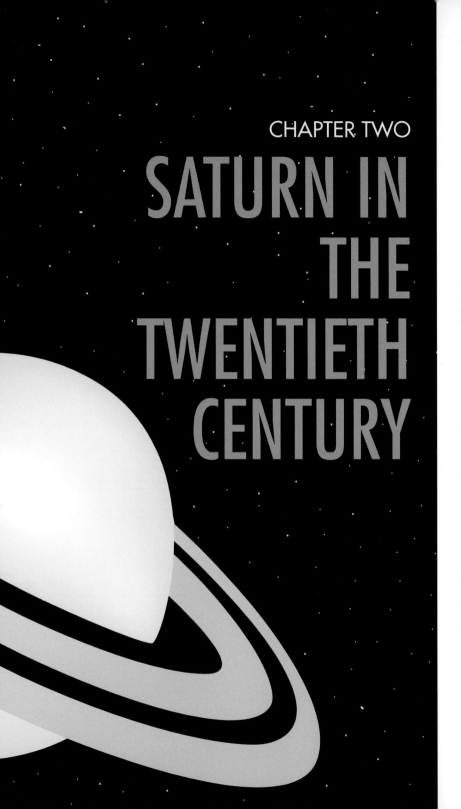

CHAPTER TWO

SATURN IN THE TWENTIETH CENTURY

Until the last decades of the twentieth century, no more was known about Saturn than could be detected through Earth-bound telescopes. Admittedly, these were a great deal more powerful than those of early centuries, but Saturn is a long way off and difficult to observe even with the best instruments. The advent of photography added a powerful new tool to astronomy, though it had its limits. Although astronomers no longer had to rely on their artistic skills to record details of the planet, the long exposures that photographs required also meant that disturbances in Earth's atmosphere were magnified.

The twinkling of stars in the sky is caused by movements in the air. It makes the stars look pretty to the naked eye, but it is an annoyance to astronomers. On a night of particularly poor visibility, the twinkling effect can make objects appear to twitch and jump, as though they were being observed through a surface of rippling water. While the human eye can catch brief moments when the atmosphere holds still and a planet or star stands out with clarity, the photographic image a camera records just keeps getting blurrier the longer it is exposed. It's like trying to photograph someone who won't hold still—you just end up with a blurry picture.

By the 1970s there were superb photos of Saturn taken by Earth-based telescopes, but few showed the detail that could be recorded by the sharp eyes of expert observers. The problem with visual observations, however, is that they are subjective—they are only as good as the person making the drawings. There is always the problem of optical illusions, lack of drawing skills, or personal prejudices. Just as witnesses to a crime will give different accounts of what they saw, no two observers of Saturn see exactly the same thing. While the camera might not be as detailed, it is at least impartially accurate.

One of the last great visual observers of Saturn was the French astronomer Bernard Lyot, who worked during the first half of the twentieth century. He discovered that there was a great deal of detailed structure in the rings. His drawings showed that the rings had countless faint, threadlike gaps. Other excellent observers, such as the French astronomer-artist Lucien Rudaux, saw other strange, elusive details, such as mysterious markings on the A ring. They looked like dusky streaks, radiating away from the planet like the spokes of a wheel.

In the first half of the twentieth century, astronomers gradually lost much of their interest in observing the planets. They thought they had discovered pretty much all that existed. While visual observers could still do valuable work recording daily changes in the planets, it didn't appear as though anything radically new could be discovered by Earth-based telescopes.

A painting of Saturn created in the 1920s by astronomer-artist Lucien Rudaux clearly shows shadowy "spokes" on the rings, a feature not confirmed until the *Voyager 1* flyby of 1980.

One of the exceptions to this was the use of the spectroscope, an instrument that can determine what elements and compounds exist on other worlds by examining the light reflected from them. The use of the spectroscope on the planets had begun in the nineteenth century, but it was not until the early decades of the twentieth century that accurate results were obtained. In 1932, a **spectrograph**—a photographic image of a spectrum examined by a spectroscope—revealed the presence of **methane** and ammonia in Saturn's atmosphere. These compounds are composed of nitrogen, carbon, and **hydrogen**. The discovery of such vast amounts of these elements on Saturn led to the first serious theory about the structure of the planet. Rupert Wildt suggested that Saturn had a small core of rock and metal surrounded by a deep layer of water, ammonia, and methane ice. Above this, he suggested, was a thick hydrogen atmosphere.

A few years later, in 1943–1944, a startling discovery was made regarding Saturn's largest moon, Titan. By studying the spectrum of the satellite, astronomer Gerard P. Kuiper found that it had a dense atmosphere of methane. It was the first moon in the solar system to have been discovered to have an atmosphere.

New satellites were also discovered, as well as a previously unknown ring. By using computer-enhanced photographs, astronomer W. A. Feibelman found an extremely faint ring outside the A ring. Only one millionth as bright as the A ring, the newly discovered E ring extends 249,000 miles (400,000 km) from Saturn.

In 1970 the first spectroscopic analysis of the composition of the rings was made, which revealed that they were mostly water

THE SPECTROSCOPE

Ordinary light is actually made up of a mixture of different colors. When light is passed through a prism, it is split up into its component colors. When this happens, a rainbowlike pattern called a **spectrum** is created. When materials are heated, they give out light—for example, the filament in a lightbulb glows brightly because it is heated by the electric current passing through it. This light can be passed through a prism to create a spectrum.

Scientists discovered that different materials create different spectra, or groups of colors, depending on the elements they consist of. It was possible, they found, to determine what elements are in a substance by examining the spectrum that is produced when the substance is heated. The instrument they use to do this is called a spectroscope.

When the spectroscope was first used on the Sun, scientists were able to learn for the first time what elements were in it. They even discovered an entirely new element, helium, which was discovered on the Sun before it was known to exist on Earth. The planets aren't hot like the Sun, however—they glow from the sunlight they reflect. But scientists can still use the spectroscope on them, because when light bounces off a surface, only some of its colors are reflected. Others are absorbed by the elements on the surface, which changes the spectrum of the reflected light. By studying these differences, scientists can determine what elements make up the planets.

ice. Other instruments gave accurate measurements of the temperature of the rings, a frigid −374°F (−190°C). This and other data led to the first accurate estimate of the size of the ring particles, which turned out to be no more than 4 to 8 inches (10 to 20 cm). The rings seemed to be made of billions of large snowballs.

All of this information represented tremendous progress, but it was pushing the limits of how much could be learned from Earth. If astronomers wanted to learn more about Saturn, they would have to go there.

CHAPTER THREE
EXPLORING SATURN

Even before the first spacecraft explored Saturn, astronomers using telescopes knew that Saturn is impressive. It is a big planet, the second largest in the solar system (only Jupiter is larger). It is 9.5 times wider than Earth and 9.5 times bigger around. If Saturn's equator were a belt that could be unfastened and stretched out straight, it would reach from Earth to the Moon. Eighty Earths could be flattened out and spread over Saturn's surface, and more than 700 planets the size of our own could be packed inside it.

The first space probe to Saturn was launched in 1973 and arrived at the ringed planet in 1979, after first making a flyby of Jupiter. Twelve instruments on the 573-pound (260-kg) *Pioneer 11* spacecraft took pictures and recorded scientific data, such as information about Saturn's **magnetic field**. The pictures were not of very good quality because the spacecraft's cameras were slow, and the fast-moving cloud formations changed too quickly for much detail to be revealed.

Voyager 1 flew past Saturn in November 1980, and *Voyager 2* in August 1981. Their cameras recorded incredible details in the planet's clouds and rings, as well as close-up photos of several of

MERCURY
VENUS
EARTH
MARS
JUPITER
SATURN
URANUS
NEPTUNE
PLUTO

A family portrait: the planets and moons of our solar system shown to the same scale as the Sun

Saturn's moons. Much of what we now know about the conditions on Saturn has come from these three spacecraft. The next mission to Saturn, the *Cassini-Huygens* probe, will arrive in 2004. One part of the spacecraft will go into orbit around Saturn, while the other will parachute down into Titan's atmosphere to make a landing on the surface.

The Anatomy of Saturn

Although Saturn is a very large planet, it is also the least massive. This is because it is made mostly of very light elements, such as hydrogen and helium. It weighs less than a ball of water the same size, which means that if you could find an ocean large enough, Saturn would float in it like a huge beach ball.

A view of the entire planet photographed by *Voyager*. [NASA]

Mass refers to how much material something is made of. **Density** refers to how tightly together the material is packed. Think of a small suitcase and a large pile of clothes. If you have a lot of clothing, you could say that the mass of the clothing is very large. But since the clothing is just lying there in a big, loose pile, the density is low. Now pack all of these clothes into the suitcase. The mass of the clothing hasn't changed—you have the same amount of clothing you started with—but now it's all been crammed into a much smaller space. The density is now a lot higher than it was before.

A **gas giant** like Saturn has a great deal of mass—much more than Earth has—but it is spread over a much larger volume than Earth, so its overall density is much lower than that of our planet. That is, an average bucketful of Saturn would weigh eight times less than an average bucketful of Earth.

Because of Saturn's low density, its surface gravity is very weak. Even though Saturn is much larger than Earth, you would only weigh slightly more there than you would on your home planet. A 150-pound (68-kg) person would weigh 160.5 pounds (73 kg) on Saturn. But this figure is an average. Because Saturn rotates so rapidly—its day is only 10 hours 39.4 minutes long—**centrifugal forces** cause objects at its equator to weigh less than they do at its poles. In fact, centrifugal forces at the equator almost cancel out the extra pull of Saturn's gravity so that you would only weigh a few ounces more than you would on Earth.

Centrifugal force has also caused Saturn to bulge at its equator. Seen through a telescope, Saturn does not look perfectly round, like our Moon, but is slightly squashed, being obviously wider than it is high. There is a difference of 7,867 miles (12,660 km) between the equatorial diameter and the polar diameter.

Saturn is 9.5 times farther away from the Sun than Earth, which means that the Sun is 9.5 times smaller in its sky. The area of the Sun would appear to be 85 times less, so that sunlight would be 85 times dimmer on Saturn than on Earth. Because Saturn is so much farther away from the Sun, it takes much longer to make one orbit. A Saturnian year is equal to 29.46 Earth years.

Inside Saturn

Astronomers believe that Saturn has a massive, molten rocky core about the size of Earth. Above this is a thick layer of metallic liquid hydrogen, and above that a layer of ordinary liquid hydrogen.

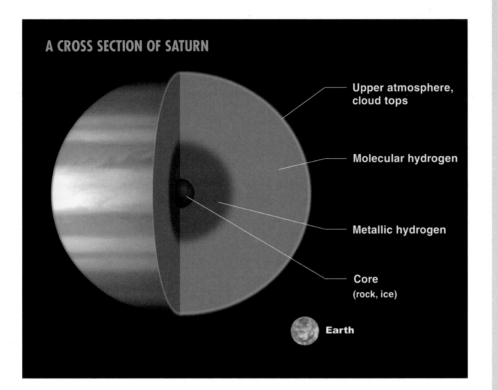

A CROSS SECTION OF SATURN

Upper atmosphere, cloud tops

Molecular hydrogen

Metallic hydrogen

Core
(rock, ice)

Earth

You've experienced centrifugal force every time you've ridden a carousel or one of the fairground rides that spins you around in a circle. The force that seems to be trying to throw you away from the center of the rotation is called centrifugal force. When a planet rotates, the material at the equator—which is the part of the planet that rotates the fastest—tries to fly away from the center. Although gravity keeps the planet from flying to pieces (which it could do if it rotated fast enough), centrifugal force is still powerful enough to cause a bulge at the equator.

Earth has an equatorial bulge caused by its rotation, though it is very slight. The difference between the equatorial diameter and the polar diameter is only about 26 miles (42 km). The difference between Saturn's equatorial diameter and its polar diameter, however, is 7,867 miles (12,660 km). It is easy to see even in a small telescope that Saturn is not spherical. The reason is that Saturn is made almost entirely of gas and liquid, which are very susceptible to distortion, while Earth is made mostly of rigid rock and metal.

This liquid hydrogen is very hot, many thousands of degrees, and under incredible pressure—millions of times the **atmospheric pressure** at the surface of Earth.

Above the layer of liquid hydrogen is a deep, gaseous atmosphere. There is probably no definite line where the liquid hydrogen ends and the atmosphere begins. Instead, the liquid hydrogen gradually becomes gaseous, without any clear-cut boundary. The

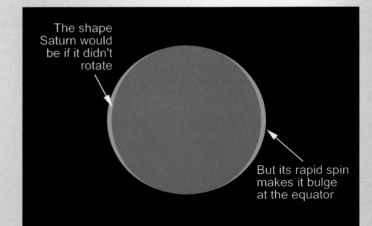

The shape Saturn would be if it didn't rotate

But its rapid spin makes it bulge at the equator

Needed: bicycle air pump

The incredible pressures deep within the core of Saturn produce vast amounts of heat. In fact, Saturn produces more heat from inside than it receives from the Sun. You can demonstrate how compression can create heat by pumping the handle of a bicycle air pump a few times and then feeling the cylinder of the pump with your hand. It will feel very warm because of the heat produced by compressing the air inside it.

Saturn's rapid rotation (its day is just 10.6 hours long) has caused its cloud belts to be stretched into long, thin bands.

(26)

atmosphere is mostly hydrogen. Six percent is helium, with only 0.0001 percent of other elements. These latter can combine with hydrogen to form many compounds, such as methane, propane, acetylene, and ammonia. These compounds freeze or liquefy, making the brightly colored clouds covering Saturn that we see from Earth.

Saturn is completely covered by clouds. No one has ever seen what lies beneath them. Seen from space, Saturn's clouds resemble those of Jupiter, complex swirling patterns stretched by the planet's rapid rotation into long streaks and bands. The resulting winds are among the most ferocious in the solar system, blowing at speeds of up to 1,060 miles an hour (1,706 km/hour). The swirling cloud patterns are cyclonic storms, like hurricanes on Earth. Unlike terrestrial hurricanes, which are powered by heat from the Sun, Saturn's storms are powered by heat created by **gravitational contraction** rising from deep inside the planet.

This is a close-up view of Saturn's cloud bands. Since Saturn is much colder than Jupiter, it doesn't have the energy to create the violent weather patterns that make Jupiter's clouds so spectacular. (The dark areas at the upper right and lower left corners were not photographed.) [NASA]

CHAPTER FOUR

THE CROWN JEWEL OF THE SOLAR SYSTEM

There is nothing in the solar system quite like Saturn's rings. Rings are not unique in themselves—Jupiter, Uranus, and Neptune all have ring systems—but there is nothing that compares to Saturn's sheer magnificence and spectacle. The rings of the other three planets are so dark and thin that they are invisible to even the most powerful telescopes—the existence of two of them was not even suspected until passing spacecraft photographed them. Saturn's, on the other hand, are brilliant—the broad B ring is brighter even than the planet itself. This is because the rings of the other planets are made of rocky dust, while Saturn's rings are made of ice. And instead of the narrow, string-like bands that form the rings of Uranus and Neptune, Saturn's are flat and wide, like a pizza or a compact disc.

The rings can be seen easily through even a small telescope. When the planet is at its maximum tilt toward or away from Earth, the rings appear brilliant white against the pale yellow planet. They are unbelievably vast. They cover an area of more than 15 billion square miles (40 billion sq km), 80 times the total surface area of Earth. To travel from the inner edge of the rings to the outer edge, a space traveler would have to cover a distance equal to 13 trips across the United States. Their full width from one side to the other is 70 percent that of the distance between Earth and the Moon. The thickness of the rings, however, rarely exceeds 33 feet (10 m). The rings are so thin that if you were to make a scale model of the rings 3 feet (1 m) wide, it would have to be 10,000 times thinner than a razor blade.

The rings are divided into three distinct bands—the outer one, the A ring, and the broader, brighter B ring. Separating them is the narrow space of the Cassini division; although, it only appears to be narrow because the rings are so large. The gap is actually large enough to drop our Moon through! Inside the B ring is the dim, translucent crêpe ring (or C ring). Even before the advent of spacecraft, astronomers were aware of at least one additional very narrow outer ring, and the *Pioneer* and *Voyager* probes discovered many more. There are now known to be at least seven distinct rings altogether. Additionally, *Voyager* found that the A and B rings are made up of 500 to 1,000 extremely narrow rings, like the grooves on an old-fashioned phonograph record.

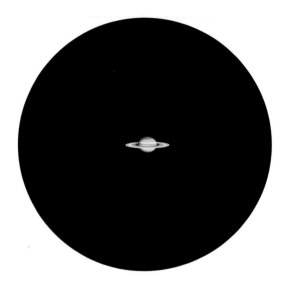

Saturn as it appears through a typical small amateur telescope

Where Did the Rings Come From?

Some astronomers believe that the rings are material that was unable to form into a moon because it lies within Saturn's Roche limit. Another idea popular among scientists suggests that during the time when Saturn was first forming, it had one or more moons just outside its Roche limit. As Saturn grew larger, its Roche limit grew, too. The limit soon moved past the inner moons.

The rings are made of billions of chunks of nearly pure water ice, similar to ice cubes. Some of the particles may be dirty or coated with dust. The ring particles are very small, ranging in size from grains of sugar to several feet. A few half-mile-sized bodies may also exist. If all of the material in the rings could be compressed into a ball, it would form a moon only 60 miles (100 km) across. Each ring particle is an individual moon and circles Saturn in its own orbit. It can rightly be said that Saturn is a planet with a billion moons.

A scene within Saturn's rings: Billions upon billions of icy chunks, ranging in size from pebbles to small houses, swirl around in a layer that is 170,500 miles (275,000 km) wide but less than 0.62 mile (1 km) thick.

These, however, were small and solid enough to avoid being pulled apart. Instead, they were shattered by **asteroids** that were being attracted to the newly formed Saturn. The remnants of these destroyed moons eventually formed the magnificent rings. There may still be large pieces of these ancient moons within the rings, much smaller than their ancestors but a thousand times larger than a typical ring particle.

The most recent theory suggests that a few hundred million years ago—at a time when the early ancestors of the dinosaurs were roaming Earth—Saturn may have had no rings at all. The rings were formed when one or more small moons wandered too close to Saturn. When they got within the Roche limit, tidal forces created by Saturn's gravity pulled them apart. After millions of years of bumping against one another, the pieces of moon were ground into the tiny particles that form the rings today.

There are many reasons that the rings are considered relatively young. One of these is how clean the ring particles are. The rings are very bright because the ice particles they are made of have not yet had time to be covered with dark dust. Another reason is that the gravitational effects of all of Saturn's moons—the same forces that create the thousands of large and small gaps in the rings— make the rings unstable. They look the way they do now only because the moons haven't had enough time yet to disrupt them. A few million years from now, however, the rings will start to fall in toward Saturn, and the solar system will lose one of its greatest natural wonders. If the rings are as short-lived as many astronomers believe them to be, we're fortunate to be here at just the right time to see them.

Facing page: Saturn's rings are a spectacular vision seen from just above the planet's cloud tops.

Between the Rings

The gaps between the rings were almost as great a mystery as the rings themselves. What makes these gaps and how are they able to remain empty of material? There are the large gaps, such as the Cassini division or the Encke division in the A ring, and the many hundreds of much smaller ones photographed by the *Voyager* probes.

The answer came in 1866 from a study of the asteroid belt by Daniel Kirkwood. Most asteroids—many hundreds of them—orbit between Mars and Jupiter. Kirkwood had noticed that they were not evenly spaced, however, but had gaps where there were few or no asteroids at all. Kirkwood realized that these gaps fell where an asteroid would have an **orbital period** (or year) that was some simple fraction of Jupiter's. For instance, if the relationship between the periods of an asteroid and Jupiter is one third, it means that every third time the asteroid goes around the Sun it lines up with Jupiter once. Each time the asteroid came close to Jupiter it would be disturbed by Jupiter's gravity. The effect of these disturbances would gradually add up, and the asteroid would be moved into a new orbit.

Kirkwood found gaps in the asteroid belt where orbital periods of asteroids would have been one third, two fifths, three sevenths, one half, and three fifths of Jupiter's. The next year, Kirkwood realized that his discovery might also be applied to the gaps in Saturn's rings. In this case, the bodies disturbing the ring particles would be the large inner moons of Saturn: Mimas, Enceladus, Tethys, and Dione.

Because the moons are so much more massive than the tiny ring particles, their effect on the particles would be very great, especially when the effects of several moons acted together. For example, a ring particle having a period one half that of Mimas, a third that of Enceladus, a quarter that of Tethys, and a sixth that of Dione would be disturbed several times a day and would be moved very quickly into a different orbit. In fact, such a particle would be within the Cassini division, so Kirkwood knew that he had found the correct explanation for the gap. Eventually, it was shown that all of the gaps in Saturn's rings can be associated with one or more of the moons.

Strange Rings

There are many mysteries associated with Saturn's rings. The *Voyager* spacecraft showed that they were not at all a simple structure. There are circular rings, eccentric rings, kinked rings, braided rings, clumpy rings, dense rings, and gossamer rings. There are ringlets and gaplets. The rings have waves, spokes, and **shepherd moons**.

The *Voyager* spacecraft discovered a narrow ring just outside the A ring. Unlike the broad, flat A and B rings, the F ring, as it was named, looks like a loop of string circling Saturn. The first pictures of the F ring astonished scientists because it looked as though it were braided from several separate strands. It also has strange kinks and lumps. Two tiny moons, Prometheus and Pandora, orbit on either side of the F ring. Their gravity may be the cause of the weird appearance of the ring as they "shepherd" the particles that form it.

Until the end of the twentieth century, Saturn's rings were thought to be unique. We now know that all of the gas giants in our solar system possess rings—Jupiter, Saturn, Uranus, and Neptune—though none are as spectacular as Saturn's. Jupiter's are dark, as thin as smoke, and have none of the complex detail of Saturn's rings. Uranus's rings are also dark, but arranged in narrow bands, like concentric loops of string. Neptune's rings resemble Uranus's narrow loops, but have strange arc-shaped clumps. All of these other rings are apparently made of dark, rocky dust. While planetary rings may have a common origin, the differences among the rings in our solar system make it clear that a great many forces are at work in forming them, some of which scientists do not yet fully understand.

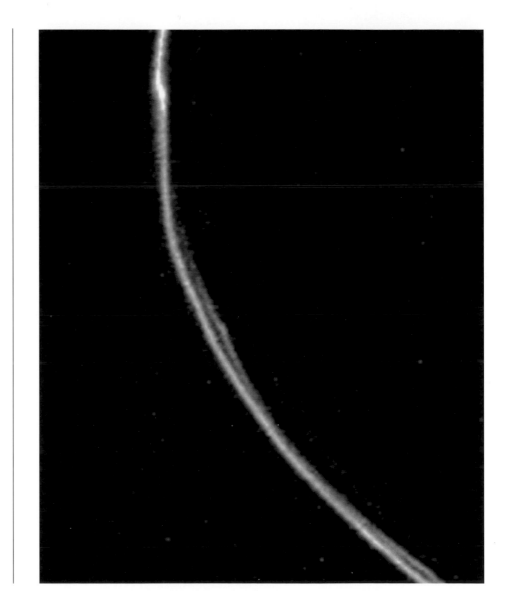

The enigmatic F ring has strange lumps and a "braided" appearance. These are probably gravitational effects caused by small moons orbiting on either side of the ring. [NASA]

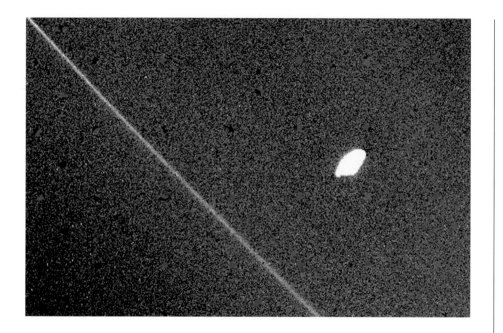

Voyager also revealed unusual spokes on the B ring (some early visual observers also recorded spokes on the rings, but these were usually dismissed as optical illusions). These look like dark shadows radiating away from the planet. They appear as a section of the ring rotates out from the shadow of Saturn, and then they gradually disappear. They form very rapidly. One spoke was seen to grow 3,728 miles (6,000 km) in only five minutes. The cause of the spokes is a mystery, but they seem to be related to Saturn's magnetic field. It may be that the magnetic field is having some sort of effect on fine particles of dust in the rings, causing them to align in patterns like iron filings on a magnet.

The strangeness of the F ring and the spokes reveals that while the rings might seem to be never-changing when seen from Earth, close up there is a great deal of action occurring. In addition to the effects of the shepherd moons and Saturn's magnetic field, the gravitational pull of Saturn and its satellites causes many other complex effects. For instance, *Voyager* discovered waves flowing back and forth across the rings, like ripples in a circular pan of water.

Facing page: The unusual "spokes" photographed by *Voyager 1* are shown here. They look like dark shadows across the rings and are most visible in the upper left area of this image. The spokes are one of the many mysteries about Saturn. [NASA]

CHAPTER FIVE

MOONS, MOONS, AND MORE MOONS

Saturn has 18 officially named satellites and 12 more recently discovered candidates. Most of them appear to be icy bodies, made mostly of water along with smaller amounts of materials such as methane, ammonia, and carbon dioxide. They range in size from giant Titan to tiny bodies only 12 miles (20 km) wide. Some of the smallest moons actually orbit within the rings themselves.

The Large Moons

Titan

Titan is the largest of Saturn's satellites and was also the first to be discovered. Christian Huygens first saw it in 1655. It is a huge body, 3,194 miles (5,140 km) in diameter, much larger than Earth's Moon. For many years it was thought that Titan was the largest moon in the solar system, but modern measurements show that Jupiter's moon, Ganymede, is slightly larger. Titan, however, is larger than the planets Pluto and Mercury, but its size is not what makes it so interesting.

In 1944, the Dutch-American astronomer Gerard P. Kuiper discovered that Titan has an atmosphere. This was an incredible and completely unexpected discovery. Until then, astronomers had assumed that all the moons in the solar system resembled our own: airless, cratered balls of rock or ice. If a moon had any atmosphere at all, it was assumed that it would be extremely thin. Titan's atmosphere, however, is surprisingly dense—much denser even than the atmosphere of our own planet. The surface pressure of the atmosphere on Titan is 50 percent greater than Earth's.

Titan's atmosphere resembles Earth's in that it is composed mostly of nitrogen—the only nitrogen-dominated atmosphere in the entire solar system other than Earth's. Unlike Earth, however, the balance of Titan's atmosphere is not oxygen. It is mostly methane, a flammable gas similar to the propane or butane burned in stoves.

Voyager found that Titan is completely covered by dense clouds. From space it looks like a blank orange ball. Sunlight acting on the chemicals in the upper atmosphere creates a photochemical smog that is too thick to see through. This smog is composed of various organic molecules, such as ethane, methane, propane, and acetylene. These compounds are usually referred to as **hydrocarbons**.

Because of the clouds, Titan's surface is completely hidden, and scientists can only guess at what it might be like. There have been some tantalizing clues from Earth-based **radar**, which can penetrate Titan's clouds, as well as from the Hubble Space Telescope (HST). The HST can record images in near-infrared

Titan's surface is hidden from view by a thick blanket of orange-colored organic molecules. [NASA]

THE MOONS OF SATURN

NAME	DATE OF DISCOVERY	DISTANCE FROM SATURN* (MILES/KILOMETERS)	SIZE† (MILES/KILOMETERS)
Pan	1990	83,008 (133,583)	6 (10)?
Atlas	1980	85,530 (137,640)	11 x 9 (18 x 14)
Prometheus	1980	86,592 (139,350)	46 x 21 (74 x 34)
Pandora	1980	88,052 (141,700)	34 x 19 (55 x 31)
Epimetheus	1966	94,094 (151,422)	43 x 33 (69 x 3)
Janus	1966	94,125 (151,472)	62 x 47 (99 x 76)
Mimas	1789	115,282 (185,520)	124 (199)
Enceladus	1789	147,906 (238,020)	155 (249)
Tethys	1684	183,102 (294,660)	329 (529)
Telesto	1980	183,102 (294,660)	9 x 5 (15 x 8)
Calypso	1980	183,102 (294,660)	9 x 5 (15 x 8)
Dione	1684	234,516 (377,400)	348 (560)
Helene	1980	234,516 (377,400)	10 (16)
Rhea	1672	327,503 (527,040)	475 (764)
Titan	1655	697,118 (1,121,850)	1,600 (2,575)
Hyperion	1848	920,356 (1,481,100)	115 x 70 (185 x 113)
Iapetus	1671	2,212,992 (3,561,300)	447 (720)

THE MOONS OF SATURN

NAME	DATE OF DISCOVERY	DISTANCE FROM SATURN (MILES/KILOMETERS)	SIZE (MILES/KILOMETERS)
S/2000 S5	2000	7,064,990 (11,370,000)	4.35 (7)?
S/2000 S6	2000	7,108,486 (11,440,000)	3.1 (5)?
Phoebe	1898	8,048,373 (12,952,000)	71 x 65 (115 x 105)
S/2000 S2	2000	9,444,982 (15,200,000)	6.2 (10)?
S/2000 S8	2000	9,724,459 (15,650,000)	1.86 (3)?
S/2000 S11	2000	10,184,274 (16,390,000)	8 (13)?
S/2000 S10	2000	10,942,347 (17,610,000)	2.5 (4)?
S/2000 S3	2000	11,284,101 (18,160,000)	9 (16)?
S/2000 S4	2000	11,333,811 (18,240,000)	4.35 (7)?
S/2000 S9	2000	11,625,855 (18,710,000)	1.86 (3)?
S/2000 S12	2000	12,098,097 (19,470,000)	1.86 (3)?
S/2000 S7	2000	12,719,468 (20,470,000)	1.86 (3)?
S/2000 S1	2000	14,353,675 (23,100,000)	5 (8)?

* As measured from the center of Saturn.

† Moons with two dimensions are not spherical. In this case, the longest and narrowest dimensions are given. Sizes with question marks are uncertain.

Titan's thick layer of dense orange clouds

Facing page: The gloomy surface of Titan, Saturn's largest moon: Heavy clouds in an atmosphere denser than Earth's prevent most of the sunlight from reaching the surface. Pools of liquid methane cover the frigid landscape. Some astronomers speculate that there may be hot springs and geysers, such as the one in the foreground.

light, which can reveal details on the surface of Titan. The resulting images show an Australia-sized bright area of rough terrain. There are also dark areas that are probably smooth. It is possible that these might be oceans of ethane. No one will know for sure until the *Huygens* probe lands.

We do know that it is very cold on the surface of Titan, with temperatures around −292°F (−180°C). Methane may exist on the surface as ice, liquid, and gas, and there may be liquid nitrogen as well. Hydrocarbons condensing out of the atmosphere may be constantly raining onto the surface, which may produce ponds and lakes of liquid hydrocarbons, such as ethane and propane. It is probably a good thing that there is no oxygen on Titan since all of the liquids that form in its atmosphere and on its surface are highly flammable!

Titan may also have volcanoes and geysers similar to those on Jupiter's Io or Neptune's Triton. These are thought to be caused by heat created deep beneath the surface, as the gravity of Saturn flexes Titan (in the same way that a rubber ball will grow warm if you repeatedly squeeze it in your hand).

It is dark beneath Titan's dense clouds. At that distance the Sun is only one ninetieth as bright as it is on Earth, and the thick haze over Titan cuts out even more light. The light level might be only about one one-thousandth that of daylight on Earth, though this will still be 350 times as bright as the moonlight on a night during a full moon.

The giant Herschel Crater dominates this view of Mimas. The crater is 80 miles (130 km) in diameter, while the entire moon is only 241 miles (390 km) in diameter. [NASA]

Facing Page: The Herschel Crater is shown here from the surface of Mimas while Saturn looms in the background.

Mimas

Mimas, the innermost of Saturn's large moons, is an icy ball 241 miles (390 km) in diameter. It is entirely covered with **craters**, but one in particular stands out. This crater, named Herschel in honor of the astronomer who discovered it in 1789, covers a third of Mimas's diameter. It was first seen in a *Voyager* photograph and was dubbed the Deathstar Crater because it made Mimas look exactly like the giant space station in the movie *Star Wars*.

Herschel Crater is about 80 miles (130 km) wide and 5.6 miles (9 km) deep. It has a high central peak that towers 13,000 feet (4 km) above the crater floor. It is about the same size as the craters Copernicus and Tycho on our own Moon, which are both about the size of Yellowstone National Park. Herschel was created by a huge impact. If it had been even a little bit larger it would probably have shattered the moon like an egg. In fact, there is evidence that this very thing may have happened in Mimas's past. It may have been struck so hard by an asteroid that it was literally blown apart and then reassembled by gravity.

The reason that Mimas is so heavily cratered is that it is so close to Saturn. The giant planet's gravity attracts many **meteoroids** and small asteroids, some of which inevitably collide with Mimas. *Voyager 2* scientists calculated that Mimas is hit twelve times more often than Saturn's outermost moon.

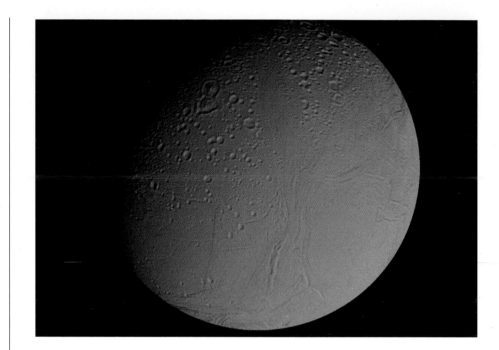

Enceladus

Enceladus is the next moon out from Mimas. It is made almost entirely of pure water ice, a fact deduced from its high reflectivity. Unlike Earth's Moon, which reflects only 11 percent of the sunlight that falls on it, Enceladus reflects almost 100 percent.

It shows evidence of considerable resurfacing. There are few craters on half of the surface, and they are relatively young ones. This means that some process has erased the older surface and replaced it. This might have been some form of ice volcanism, where melted ice flowed over the surface like lava.

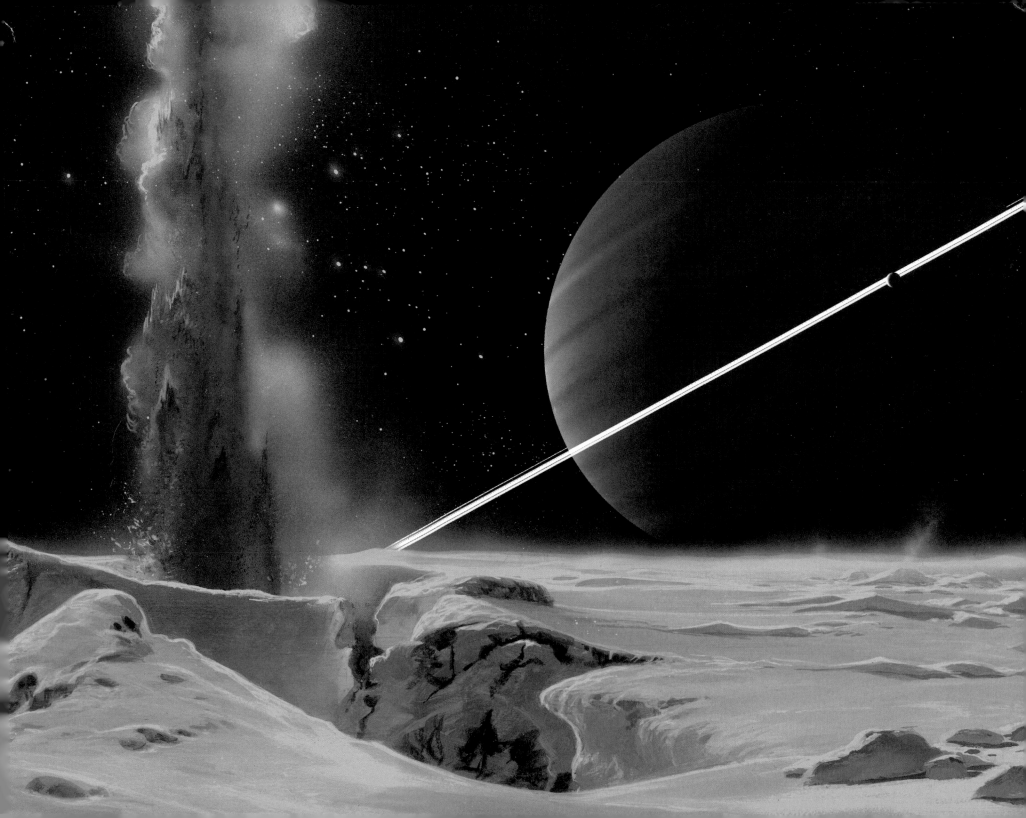

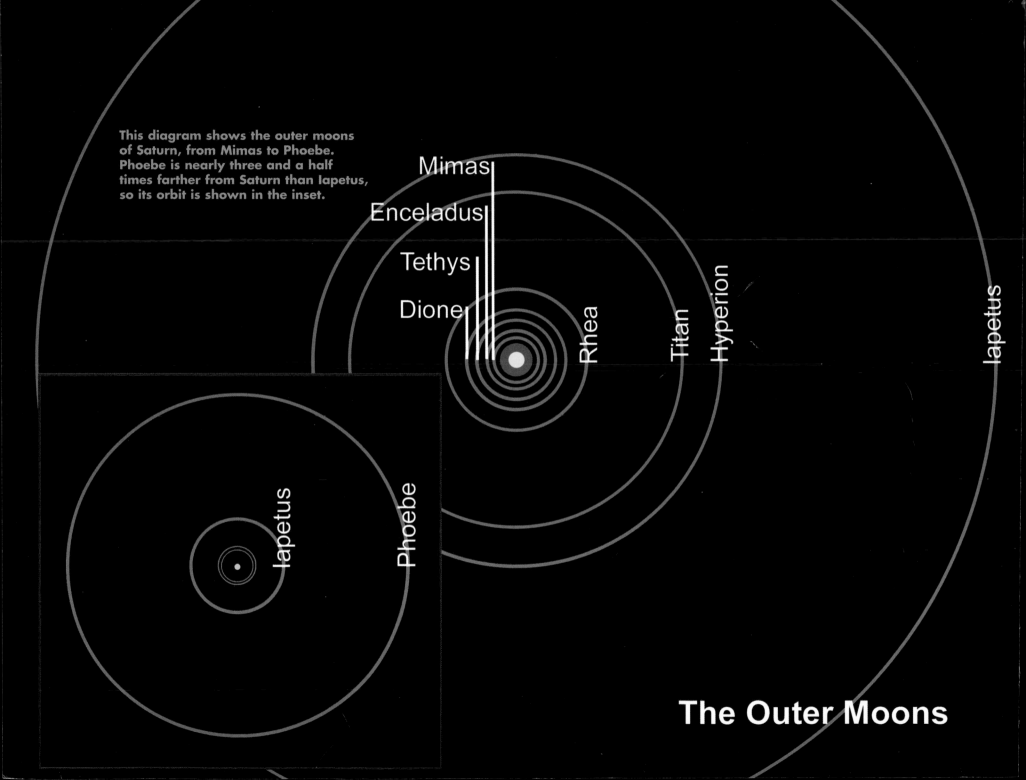

This diagram shows the outer moons of Saturn, from Mimas to Phoebe. Phoebe is nearly three and a half times farther from Saturn than Iapetus, so its orbit is shown in the inset.

Mimas

Enceladus

Tethys

Dione

Rhea

Titan

Hyperion

Iapetus

Iapetus

Phoebe

The Outer Moons

Tethys

Unlike Enceladus, Tethys is covered with impact craters such as Odysseus, one of the largest known impact structures in the solar system. It is 248 miles (400 km) wide—two fifths the width of the satellite. It was probably prevented from completely shattering Tethys because it may have hit the moon when Tethys was still not completely formed. Because Tethys was not yet quite solid, it absorbed the impact instead of breaking up. Odysseus is very flat, its rim hardly rising above the surrounding terrain. This is because Tethys is mostly ice, and ice will flow with time, in the same way that glaciers will slowly flow down a mountain. Craters and mountains on icy worlds will therefore tend to flatten out over thousands of years.

In addition to Odysseus, Tethys also boasts a huge valley called Ithaca Chasma. It is 62 miles (100 km) wide and 2 to 3 miles (3 to 5 km) deep. It stretches for 1,243 miles (2,000 km), three quarters of the way around the satellite. It may be the remnant of a vast crack in the surface created by the impact that caused Odysseus.

A photograph of Tethys from *Voyager 2* shows Ithaca Chasma, an enormous trench that stretches diagonally across the middle of the satellite. It may have been created at the same time as the impact that created Odysseus, the large crater at the upper right.

Tethys features an enormous canyon called Ithaca Chasma that stretches two thirds of the way around the small moon.

Like most of Saturn's moons, Dione is covered with vast plains of ice. The bright streaks along the right edge may be faults exposing fresh ice. (The grid of black dots was created by the spacecraft's camera to allow astronomers to detect distortions in the photograph.) [NASA]

Facing page: Saturn as seen from the surface of Dione

Dione

Dione, discovered in 1684 by Cassini, is about the same size as Tethys, but denser. In fact, it is the densest of all Saturn's moons, with the exception of Titan. This means that it probably has a large amount of rock mixed with its ice. One hemisphere has a network of bright streaks on a dark surface with only a few craters. The streaks are clearly newer than the craters because they fall on top of them. The opposite hemisphere is heavily cratered and even brighter.

Astronomers believe that Dione was probably volcanically active in the past because much of it has been resurfaced. This might have produced the streaks, and then a new series of impacts might have occurred. Since Dione keeps one face permanently locked onto Saturn, one hemisphere leads and the other trails as the satellite orbits around the planet. Just as more bugs will splatter on the front windshield of a car than on the back window, more meteoroids hit the leading side of Dione than the trailing side. These impacts wiped out most of the effects of the volcanism, such as light streaks, on that side of the moon but left the other side untouched.

Rhea

Rhea is similar in appearance to Dione, with bright, wispy streaks covering one hemisphere. It is heavily cratered with several winding, narrow trenches. Rhea is only about half the size of our Moon. Like many of Saturn's moons, it is made mostly of ice, with a little darker material mixed in. Its extremely low density implies that Rhea might best be described as a giant snowball. The surface of Rhea probably resembles creamy white, finely crushed ice because of the effect of millions of years of erosion by tiny meteorites—called **micrometeorites**—smaller than grains of sand.

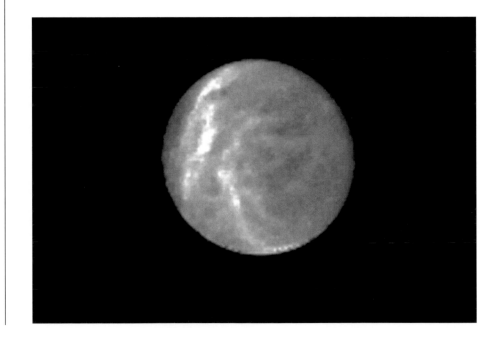

Bright streaks and blotches on the surface of Rhea may be the result of pulverized ice thrown from impact craters.

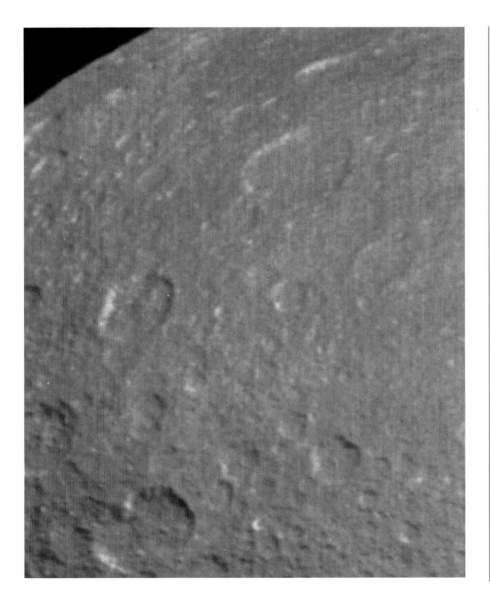

Multiple impact craters can be seen on the ancient, icy surface of Rhea. [NASA/JPL]

A close-up view of Rhea: The bright rims on some of the craters may be exposed ice. [NASA]

Saturn, seen from the surface of Rhea,
is 520,000 miles (837,000 km) away.

Astronomers had long been puzzled by the changes in the brightness of Iapetus. *Voyager* discovered that the reason for this is the two-tone surface of the satellite. One half is covered with bright ice, like most of Saturn's other moons, but the other half is covered with some undetermined dark material. [NASA]

Facing page: Here we see Saturn from the dark face of Iapetus.

Iapetus

Iapetus may be one of the strangest moons in the solar system. Cassini discovered it in 1671 and noticed something very puzzling. When Iapetus was on one side of Saturn it was very bright, but when it went halfway around in its orbit and was on the other side of Saturn, it was almost invisible! Cassini soon figured out what was going on. He reasoned that Iapetus kept one side always facing toward Saturn, just as our Moon always keeps one face toward Earth. This meant that when Iapetus was on one side of Saturn he saw the leading hemisphere, and when it was on the other side he saw the trailing hemisphere. If the leading side of the satellite was much darker than the trailing side, this would explain why Iapetus seemed to change its brightness so radically.

Voyager showed that Cassini was right. One side of Iapetus is more than ten times darker than the other. It is covered with a reddish-brown soil that is almost as dark as black velvet. The line between the bright side and dark side is very sharply defined. Why Iapetus has such mismatched hemispheres is a mystery.

One possible explanation involves Phoebe, the next and farthest moon out. Unlike all of Saturn's other moons, it orbits in a **retrograde** direction, which means that it circles Saturn in the opposite direction of the other satellites. It is also covered with a dark gray soil. Any of this blown off by meteorite impacts would spiral in toward Saturn. Some would run into Iapetus. Since the dust and Iapetus would be traveling in opposite directions, the dust would impact the leading hemisphere of the moon at a very high speed. Not only would that side of Iapetus get coated with

dark material, the impact would also tend to vaporize the ice in Iapetus's soil, leaving even more dark material behind.

The only problem with this theory is that the dark coating on Iapetus is the wrong color. Phoebe's soil is a dark, neutral gray, whereas the coating on Iapetus is reddish brown. It might be that chemical reactions between the dust and ice are caused by the heat of impact. These reactions might create reddish organic compounds. Another possibility is that the reddish-brown material was erupted volcanically from within Iapetus.

The Small Moons

In addition to its half-dozen large, icy moons, Saturn has many small satellites. These are all made of ice and are too small to be round. Gravity pulls a moon or planet into a spherical shape. But if a moon is very small, the ice or rock it's made of is stronger than its force of gravity. Small moons like these can be almost any shape.

These small moons are as unusual as their bigger cousins. Some types of moons are found only in the Saturn system and nowhere else. These include the shepherd satellites, the **co-orbitals**, and the **Lagrangian satellites**.

There are three shepherd satellites: Atlas, Pandora, and Prometheus. They are called shepherd satellites because of their close relationship with Saturn's rings. Orbiting on either side of the narrow F ring, like shepherds herding a flock of sheep, the combined effect of the gravity of Pandora and Prometheus is probably the cause of the ring's strange braided, kinked shape. Pan, the 18th and most recently named satellite, orbits within the A ring and helps clear the Encke division of particles.

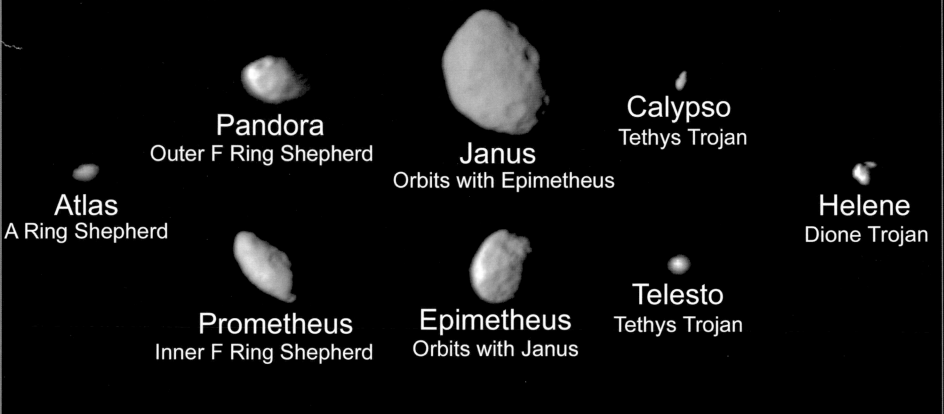

Atlas
A Ring Shepherd

Pandora
Outer F Ring Shepherd

Janus
Orbits with Epimetheus

Calypso
Tethys Trojan

Helene
Dione Trojan

Prometheus
Inner F Ring Shepherd

Epimetheus
Orbits with Janus

Telesto
Tethys Trojan

The innermost moons of Saturn are very small—too small, in fact, to be round. [NASA]

The co-orbital satellites, Janus and Epimetheus, orbit at almost exactly the same distance from Saturn, on the outer fringe of the rings. Every four years the inner satellite, which orbits slightly faster, approaches the slower-moving outer satellite. Instead of colliding, however, the moons exchange orbits. The outer moon becomes the inner moon and vice versa. Then the whole four-year cycle begins again. Astronomers think that they might once have been a single satellite that broke in half.

In the orbit of every moon or planet there are points 60 degrees ahead of an object and 60 degrees behind in which a smaller object can remain in a stable position. The **Trojan** asteroids, for instance, lie in the same orbit as Jupiter, 60 degrees ahead of the planet and 60 degrees behind. These stable areas are called the Lagrangian points, after Joseph-Louis Lagrange, the French astronomer who first worked out their mathematics. Saturn's Lagrangian satellites, Calypso, Helene, and Telesto, orbit in the same paths as the larger moons. Two are in the same orbit as Tethys, and one is in the same orbit as Dione.

Hyperion

Hyperion is a small moon that orbits between Titan and Iapetus. It is made of ice mixed with rocky material, which accounts for its dark color. Although it is not much smaller than Mimas, it has a highly irregular shape. This, along with its battered appearance, suggests that it might once have been part of a larger body that was broken up in a catastrophic collision. Its chaotic tumbling rotation supports the idea that something large once hit it.

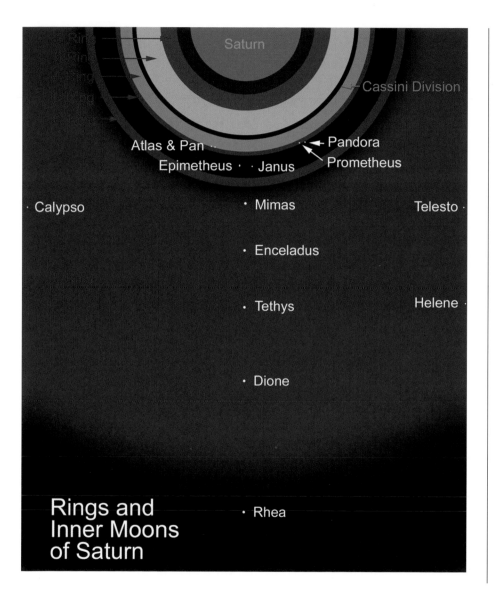

Saturn

Cassini Division

Atlas & Pan ·   · ← Pandora
Epimetheus · · Janus   Prometheus

· Calypso   · Mimas   Telesto ·

· Enceladus

· Tethys   Helene ·

· Dione

**Rings and
Inner Moons
of Saturn**   · Rhea

Saturn's rings and inner moons: Telesto and Calypso are Trojan satellites that share the same orbit as Enceladus, while Helene is a Trojan satellite of Dione. Janus and Epimetheus share the same orbit. Atlas and Pan, and Pandora and Prometheus, are shepherd moons that orbit within the rings themselves.

Phoebe

Phoebe is the most distant of all Saturn's major moons. Its dark color is similar to that of **carbonaceous** asteroids—that is, asteroids that have a great deal of carbon in their makeup. This, along with Phoebe's highly inclined retrograde orbit, which is unlike that of any of Saturn's other moons, suggests that it might be a captured asteroid—perhaps one that wandered into Saturn's gravitational field. Also unlike every other Saturnian satellite, except Hyperion, Phoebe does not keep one face locked onto the planet. It has a rotation period of about nine hours. Although it is smaller than irregularly shaped Hyperion, Phoebe is spherical.

CHAPTER SIX

THE FUTURE OF SATURN

Saturn has already been explored by several spacecraft—*Pioneer 11* in 1979 and *Voyagers 1* and *2* in 1980 and 1981. On its way to the ringed planet is a new robot explorer, the Cassini-Huygens mission, which reaches Saturn in 2004. Unlike the previous encounters, which flew by the planet at thousands of miles an hour, the *Cassini-Huygens* spacecraft will go into orbit around Saturn. Instead of being able to observe the planet for only a few minutes, *Cassini-Huygens* will remain in orbit for years.

The *Cassini-Huygens* spacecraft, which was launched in 1997, weighs 12,346 pounds (5,600 kg) and stands 22.3 feet (6.8 m) tall, making it the largest interplanetary probe ever sent from Earth. The spacecraft actually consists of two parts: the *Cassini* orbiter and the *Huygens* lander, which will separate from the orbiter and descend to the surface of Titan.

The Cassini-Huygens mission is an international effort. In addition to the involvement of the United States, many other countries have contributed instruments, software, and scientific investigators. These international partners include Austria, Belgium, the Czech Republic, Denmark, the European Space

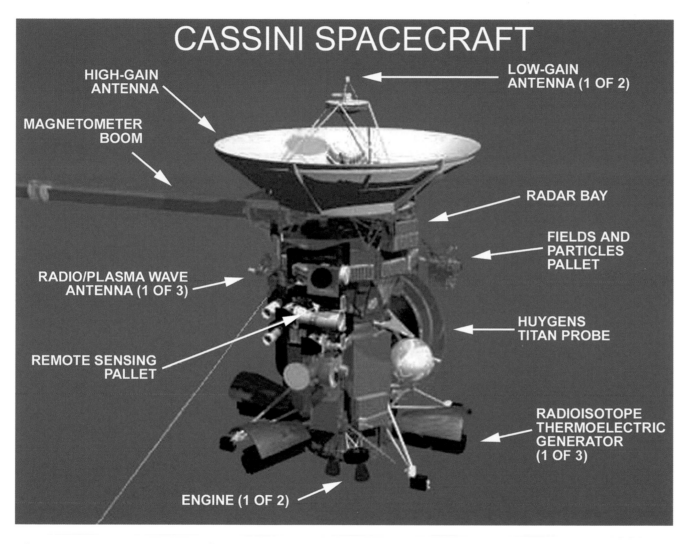

CASSINI SPACECRAFT

HIGH-GAIN ANTENNA

LOW-GAIN ANTENNA (1 OF 2)

MAGNETOMETER BOOM

RADAR BAY

FIELDS AND PARTICLES PALLET

RADIO/PLASMA WAVE ANTENNA (1 OF 3)

HUYGENS TITAN PROBE

REMOTE SENSING PALLET

RADIOISOTOPE THERMOELECTRIC GENERATOR (1 OF 3)

ENGINE (1 OF 2)

The *Cassini-Huygens* spacecraft

Agency, Finland, France, Germany, Hungary, Ireland, Italy, the Netherlands, Norway, Spain, Sweden, Switzerland, and the United Kingdom.

The *Cassini* spacecraft carries 12 instruments consisting of 27 different sensors. Among these instruments are cameras that will photograph the planet and its moons. These will also provide the first detailed close-up images of the rings. Several different spectrometers will allow scientists to study the structure and composition of the rings, the composition and behavior of Saturn's atmosphere, and the composition of many of the moons.

The spacecraft will study Titan's surface using radar, since the surface cannot be seen through thick cloud cover. Scientists will be able to use it to map the surface of the satellite and determine whether there are any large bodies of liquid. A radio science instrument will measure the temperatures and electrical fields of Saturn and its moons. A cosmic dust analyzer will study the ice and dust particles in the Saturn system, enabling scientists to study the chemical composition of the rings. A magnetometer will measure the magnetic field of Saturn.

The *Huygens* lander carries six instruments consisting of 39 sensors that will measure the structure and composition of Titan's atmosphere, its winds, temperature, and pressure. Various cameras will record the descent to the surface.

Human Exploration

Will human beings ever visit Saturn and its moons? It is possible, and it may be that Saturn will be visited before Jupiter, even

A last look at Saturn as the *Voyager* spacecraft was departing. A crescent Saturn had never been seen before, since the giant planet is more distant from the Sun than Earth. [NASA]

though Saturn is nearly twice as far from Earth. There are two reasons for this. The first is that Saturn doesn't appear to have the dangerous radiation fields that surround Jupiter, which would be fatal to human explorers of that planet or even its nearest moons.

But there is an even better reason. The giant planets are very far from Earth—Jupiter is 483,636,000 miles (778,300,000 km) from the Sun, and Saturn is 888,230,000 miles (1,429,400,000 km). A spacecraft carrying humans that far requires a great deal of fuel—not just for the trip out but, probably more importantly, for the trip home as well. What if there was some way to refuel a spaceship at the end of its outward journey? If that could be done, then it would have to carry only half the fuel, which means that even less fuel would be required at the start of the trip. Not only does the weight of the spaceship need to be launched from Earth, but the weight of the fuel must also be lifted.

There *is* a kind of "gas station" in orbit around Saturn, one where a spaceship could refuel for the trip back to Earth—or, perhaps, even farther out into the solar system, to Uranus, Neptune, or beyond. This gas station is Titan. Its atmosphere contains vast amounts of methane, a highly flammable gas. Compressed into a liquid and pumped into a spaceship's tanks, it would make an excellent rocket fuel. The only element required to burn it would be oxygen, which the spaceship can either carry from Earth or obtain from the ice in Saturn's rings or even one of its small moons.

Perhaps Saturn not only will be the goal of future astronauts but also the gateway to the rest of the solar system.

asteroid: a rocky or metallic interplanetary body, usually larger than 33 feet (10 m).

atmospheric pressure: the weight of a planet's atmosphere on the surface.

carbonaceous: describes minerals containing carbon.

centrifugal force: the tendency of a body rotating around a center to fly off on a tangent.

co-orbitals: satellites that orbit the same distance from a planet.

crater: the hole excavated by the impact of a meteor or asteroid onto a planet or moon.

density: how closely packed the material is in an object; the proportion of mass to volume.

ecliptic: the plane of Earth's orbit projected onto the sky; approximately, the plane of the solar system.

gas giant: a large planet composed primarily of gases and liquids.

gravitational contraction: the process by which gravity causes the material at the center of a body to become more densely packed. This usually creates heat.

hydrocarbon: an organic compound, such as acetylene or butane, consisting of combinations of hydrogen and carbon only.

hydrogen: the simplest, lightest, and most abundant element in the universe.

Langrangian satellites: satellites that occupy the gravitationally stable positions that lie 60 degrees ahead of or behind a planet in its orbit.

magnetic field: the electromagnetic field surrounding a magnet.

mass: the amount of material in an object.

meteoroid, meteor, meteorite: A *meteoroid* is a small rocky or metallic body. A *meteor*

(73)

is the streak of light seen in the sky when a meteoroid strikes the atmosphere and burns up. A *meteorite* is a meteoroid after it has landed on the surface of a planet. The word *meteor* is often used interchangeably for all three meanings.

methane: a flammable hydrocarbon gas.

micrometeorite: a very small meteor, the size of a particle of dust.

orbit: the path taken by a satellite circling a planet or the Sun.

orbital period: the length of time it takes a satellite to orbit its planet or a planet to orbit the Sun.

radar: from "radio detection and ranging," it is a method for measuring the distance to an object by bouncing radio waves from it and timing how long it takes the waves to return. It can also be used to determine the smoothness or roughness of a surface.

retrograde: the clockwise orbit of a planet or moon or rotation of a body as seen from over its north pole.

Roche limit: the closest distance a large body can approach a planet without tidal forces pulling it apart.

satellite: from the Greek word meaning "companion," any object orbiting another one.

shepherd moons: small satellites that orbit on either side of a planet's ring; their gravity helps to keep the ring in place or maintain its shape.

spectrograph: a photographic image of a spectrum examined by a spectroscope.

spectroscope: an instrument that records a photographic image of a spectrum.

spectrum: the rainbow of colors that forms when light is passed through a prism.

tidal force: the effect of an uneven pull of gravity, which does not act equally over an object. The part of an object that is farthest away is pulled on less than the side that is closest. This unequal pull can cause stresses, which, if strong enough, can cause volcanic eruptions or even tear the smaller body apart.

Trojan: a satellite occupying one of a planet's Lagrangian points.

Books

Beatty, J. Kelly, Carolyn Collins Petersen, and Andrew Chaikin, eds. *The New Solar System*. Cambridge, MA: Sky Publishing Corp, 1999.

Hartmann, William K. *Moons and Planets*. Belmont, CA: Wadsworth Publishing Co., 1999.

Kallen, Stuart A. *Exploring the Origins of the Universe*. Brookfield, CT: Twenty-First Century Books, 1997.

Miller, Ron, and William K. Hartmann. *The Grand Tour*. New York: Workman Publishing Co., 1993.

Scagell, Robine. *The New Book of Space*. Brookfield, CT: Copper Beech, 1997.

Schaaf, Fred. *Planetology*. Danbury, CT: Franklin Watts, 1996.

Silverstein, Alvin, Virginia Silverstein, and Laura Silverstein Nunn. *The Universe*. Brookfield, CT: Twenty-First Century Books, 2003.

Spangenburger, Ray, Kit Moser, and Diane Moser. *A Look at Saturn*. Danbury, CT: Franklin Watts, 2001.

Spilker, Linda J., ed. *Passage to a Ringed World*. Washington, DC: National Aeronautics and Space Administration, 1997.

Magazines

Astronomy
www.astronomy.com

Sky & Telescope
www.skypub.com

Online

Alpha Centauri's Universe
www.to-scorpio.com/index.htm
A good site for basic information about the solar system.

Cassini–Huygens Mission
Homepage
www.jpl.nasa.gov/cassini/
Information about the next
spacecraft to visit Saturn.

NASA Spacelink
spacelink.msfc.nasa.gov/index.
html
Gateway to many NASA Web
sites about the Sun and planets.

Nine Planets
www.nineplanets.org
Detailed information about
the Sun, the planets, and all
the moons, including many
photos and useful links to
other Web sites.

Planet Orbits
www.alcyone.de
A free software program that
allows the user to see the positions of all the planets in the
solar system at one time.

Planet's Visibility
www.alcyone.de
A free software program that
allows users to find out when
they can see a particular planet
and where to look in the sky.

Solar System Simulator
space.jpl.nasa.gov/
An amazing Web site that
allows the visitor to travel to
all the planets and moons and
create their own views of
these distant worlds.

Voyager Project Homepage
vraptor.jpl.nasa.gov/voyager/
voyager.html
Official site for information
about the Voyager 1 and 2
missions.

Organizations

American Astronomical
Society
2000 Florida Avenue NW
Suite 400
Washington, DC 20009-1231
www.AAS.org

Association of Lunar and
Planetary Observers
P.O. Box 171302
Memphis, TN 38187-1302
www.lpl.arizona.edu/alpo/

Astronomical Society of the
Pacific
390 Ashton Avenue
San Francisco, CA 94112
www.astrosociety.org

The Planetary Society
65 N. Catalina Avenue
Pasadena, CA 91106
planetary.org

Gravitational contraction, 27
Gravity, 25, 62

Helene, 42–43, *63*, 64, *65*
Helium, 19, 23, 27
Herschel, Sir John, 12
Herschel, Sir William, 12, *13*, 13
Herschel Crater, *46*, 46, *47*
Hevelius, *9*
Hubble Space Telescope (HST), 41
Huygens, Christian, *9*, 9–12, 40
Hydrocarbons, 41, 44
Hydrogen, 19, 23–25, 27
Hyperion, 12, 42–43, *50*, 64, 66

Iapetus, 12, 42–43, *50*, 60, *60*, *61*, 62, 64
Io, 44
Ithaca Chasma, *51*, 51, *52–53*

Janus, 42–43, *63*, 64, *65*
Jupiter, 34, 64, 70, 71
   clouds, 27
   name of, 7
   rings of, 28, 35

Keeler, James E., 15

Kirkwood, Daniel, 34–35
Kuiper, Gerard P., 19, 41

Lagrange, Joseph-Louis, 64
Lagrangian points, 64
Lagrangian satellites, 62, 64
Laplace, Pierre-Simon, 12–13
Louis XIV, King of France, 11, 12
Lyot, Bernard, 17

Magnetic field, 21, 39
Mars, 7, 34
Mass, 24
Maxwell, James Clerk, 15
Mercury, 7
Meteoroids, 46, 54
Mcthanc, 19, 27, 41, 44, 72
Micrometeorites, 56
Mimas, 12, 34, 35, 42–43, 46, *47*, *50*, 64, *65*
Moon, Earth's, 46, 48
Moons of Saturn, 11, 12, 19, 34–35, 40–67, *42–43*

Neptune, rings of, 28, 35
Newton, Isaac, 5
Nitrogen, 19

Odysseus Crater, 51
Orbital period, 34

Pan, 42–43, 62, *65*
Pandora, 35, 42–43, 62, *63*, *65*
Phoebe, *50*, 60, 62, 66, *67*
Pioneer 11 spacecraft, 21, 29, 68
Prometheus, 35, 42–43, 62, *63*, *65*
Propane, 27, 41, 44

Radar, 41
Retrograde motion, 60, 66
Rhea, 12, 42–43, *50*, 56, *56*, *57*, *58–59*, *65*
Riccioli, Giambattista, *9*
Rings
   of Jupiter, Uranus, and Neptune, 28, 35
   of Saturn, 9–15, *10*, 17, *18*, 19–20, 28–29, *30*, *31*, 32, *33*, 34–35, *36*, 37, *37*, *38*, 39, *65*
Roche, Édouard, 13–14
Roche limit, 13–14, 29, 32
Rudaux, Lucien, 17, 18

Saturn, *29*
   anatomy of, 23–24

Hugo Award-winner Ron Miller is an illustrator and author who specializes in astronomy. He has created or contributed to many books on the subject, including *Cycles of Fire*, *The History of Earth*, and *The Grand Tour*. Among his nonfiction books for young people are *The History of Rockets* and *The History of Science Fiction*, as well as the Worlds Beyond series, including *Extrasolar Planets*, *The Sun*, *Jupiter*, *Venus*, *Earth and the Moon*, *Uranus and Neptune*, and *Mercury and Pluto*. Miller's work has won many awards and distinctions, including the 2002 Hugo Award for Best Non-Fiction for *The Art of Chesley Bonestell*. He has designed a set of ten commemorative stamps on the planets in our solar system for the U.S Postal Service. He has written several novels and has worked on a number of science-fiction films, such as *Dune* and *Total Recall*. His original paintings can be found in collections all over the world, including that of the National Air and Space Museum in Washington D.C., and magazines such as *National Geographic*, *Scientific American*, *Sky & Telescope*, and *Natural History*. Miller lives in King George, Virginia, with his wife and five cats.